Alligators

Patricia Kendell

RAINTREE
STECK-VAUGHN
PUBLISHERS

A Harcourt Company

Austin   New York
www.raintreesteckvaughn.com

Alligators Chimpanzees Dolphins
Elephants Gorillas Grizzly Bears
Leopards Lions Pandas
Polar Bears Sharks Tigers

Published by Raintree Steck-Vaughn Publishers, an imprint of Steck-Vaughn Company

Library of Congress Cataloging-in-Publication Data available upon request

ISBN 0-7398-5495-X

Printed in Hong Kong. Bound in the United States.

1 2 3 4 5 6 7 8 9 0 LB 06 05 04 03 02

Photograph acknowledgements:
Bruce Coleman 20 & cover, 21, 22;
FLPA 15 (Albert Visage), 24 (David Hosking), 14 (Fritz Polking), 13 & 32 (Winifried Wisniewski);
NHPA 4 (E A Janes), 28 (Joe Blossom), 16 (Martin Harvey);
OSF 1, 7, 17 & 19 (Philippe Henry), 8, 9, 12 & 18 (Stan Osolinski);
Science Photo Library 6 (Treat Davidson0, 10 (Sam Fried), 11 (Jeff Lepore), 26 (M H Sharp);
Still Pictures 29 (Yves Lefevre), 25 (Michel Roggo), 27 (K Schafer – Peter Arnold Inc), 23 (Roland Seitre), 5 (Norbert Wu).

Contents

Where Alligators Live

Alligators live in rivers, lakes, and marshy places in parts of the United States and China. There are very few Chinese alligators left.

Alligators are closely related to crocodiles, which live
in Africa, Australia, and in other parts of the world.

5

Baby Alligators

A female alligator makes a mound of mud
and plants in a place that will not be **flooded**.
She lays her eggs here.

The babies begin to break out of the eggs. They make a croaking sound. When the mother hears this, she will help them out of the nest.

Looking After the Babies

When the eggs have **hatched**, the mother
alligator carries her babies to the water.
There, they will be safe and warm.

This baby alligator stays close to its mother.
She will make sure that it is not harmed.

Enemies

When they are small, the babies have many enemies, such as this heron.

Raccoons also find that baby alligators
make a tasty meal.

Growing Up

Alligators will stay with their mother for at least one year. They leave when the mother starts to make a new nest.

This young American alligator is now big
enough to live on its own.

Keeping in Touch

Alligators "talk" to each other in many ways. They make **bellowing** noises that can be heard 150 meters away.

They can send messages through water. They blow
bubbles, or slap the water with their heads.

Keeping Warm

Lying in the sun helps an alligator to keep its blood at the right **temperature**.

When it gets too hot, alligators slip into the water
to cool down.

Getting Around

Alligators are excellent swimmers. They can close their **nostrils** when they are under the water. They can open them on the **surface** to breathe.

On land, alligators crawl or walk. They can even **gallop** for a short **distance**.

Jaws and Teeth

Alligators can snap their jaws shut
with great force.

As their teeth wear down, new teeth grow in place of the old ones. An alligator can have many new sets of teeth during its life.

Food All Around

Young alligators eat mainly insects, snails, and small fish.

An adult alligator, like this black caiman,
will try to kill any large animal it can find,
such as a turtle or a wild pig.

In for the Kill!

Alligators hide in the water and watch for **prey**.
The alligators are very difficult to spot.

This alligator has caught a piranha fish.
Sometimes, alligators leap out of the water
to catch a bird.

Alligators in Danger

The main **threat** to alligators is the loss of the wet places where they live.

People kill alligators to stop them from
taking farm animals. Alligators are also
killed to use their skins for leather.

Helping Alligators to Survive

The few Chinese alligators left are being looked after in special protected ponds.

If laws are made to stop people hunting alligators and the wet places where they live are looked after, more alligators will survive in the future.

Further Information

ORGANIZATIONS TO CONTACT

World Wildlife Fund
1250 Twenty-Fourth Street, N.W.
P.O. Box 97180
Washington, D.C. 20077-7180

The Wildlife Society
5410 Grosveenor Lane
Bethesda, MD 20814

Care For the Wild
P.O. Box 46250
Madison, WI 53744-6250

BOOKS

Arnosky, Jim. *All About Alligators*. New York: Scholastic Trade, 1994.

Berger, Melvin. *Snap!: A Book About Alligators and Crocodiles (Hello Reader)*. New York: Cartwheel Books, 2002.

Fowler, Allan. *Gator or Croc? (Rookie Read-About Science)*. San Francisco, CA: Children's Book Press, 1997.

Simon, Seymour. *Crocodiles and Alligators*. New York: HarperCollins Publishers, 1999.

Glossary

WEBSITES

Most young children will need adult help when visiting websites. Those listed have child-friendly pages to bookmark.

http://www.animal.discovery.com
This site has video sequences of alligators and crocodiles.

http://home.cfl.rr.com/gatorhole
Provides information suitable for more able readers with links to interesting photographs suitable for all ages.

bellowing – **(BEL-oh-ing)** to shout or roar

distance – **(DISS-tuhnss)** the amount of space between two places

flooded – **(FLUHD-ed)** when water rises too high

gallop – **(GAL-uhp)** to run

hatched – **(HACHD)** when a baby animal has broken out of its shell

nostrils – **(NOSS-truhls)** the openings on an animal's nose that let in the air

prey – **(PRAY)** an animal hunted by another animal for food

surface – **(SUR-fiss)** the top of something, in this case the water

temperature – **(TEM-pur-uh-chur)** the degree of heat or cold in something

threat – **(THRET)** danger

Index

B
babies 6-11
breathe 18

C
crawl 19
crocodiles 5

E
eat 22
eggs 6, 7

G
gallop 19

H
heron 10

J
jaws 20

K
kill 23, 27

L
laws 29

M
messages 15
mother 7, 8, 9, 11

N
nest 7, 12
noises 14

P
ponds 28
prey 24

R
raccoon 11
S
skin 27
swim 18

T
talk 14
teeth 21

W
walk 19
water 15, 17, 18,
   24, 25